Editor
Nancy Hoffman

Managing Editor
Karen J. Goldfluss, M.S. Ed.

Cover Artist
Brenda DiAntonis

Art Production Manager
Kevin Barnes

Art Coordinator
Renée Christine Yates

Imaging
Rosa C. See

Publisher
Mary D. Smith, M.S. Ed.

Spotlight On
AMERICA

Grades 5 & Up

The Great Depression

JOBLESS MEN
KEEP GOING
WE CAN'T TAKE CARE OF OUR OW
CHAMBER OF COMMER

Author

Robert W. Smith

Teacher Created Resources, Inc.
6421 Industry Way
Westminster, CA
www.teachercreat
ISBN-1-4206-3
©2006 Teacher Created
Made in U.S.

Teacher
Created
Resources

D1401926

Table of Contents

Introduction

The *Spotlight on America* series is designed to introduce some of the significant events in American history to students. Reading in the content area is enriched with a variety of activities in written language, literature, social studies, oral expression, science, and mathematics. The series is designed to make history literally come alive in your classroom and take root in the minds of your students.

The Great Depression was a transforming event in American history. In the decades before the Depression, there was a growing movement to unionize industrial workers because of low wages and poor treatment by companies. The collapse of the economy, combined with the federal government's ineffective action, led to a radical change in attitudes about businesses.

The New Deal was initiated by President Franklin D. Roosevelt to resolve the economic crisis in the United States. It attempted to confront three critical problems. First, it funneled federal money into direct relief for the needy. It also stimulated the growth of the economy by providing jobs and income to the unemployed through construction projects and other jobs. Lastly, it sought to prevent future depressions by correcting the problems and unfairness of the present system. New Deal programs tried to enforce fairness in stock sales and encourage equitable treatment of workers. Social Security, a nationwide retirement system, was created. New Deal programs radically altered the American economy and provided special help to farmers, workers, immigrants, blacks, and others who had not always shared in times of prosperity.

The reading selections and comprehension questions in this book introduce the Great Depression and set the stage for activities in other subject areas. The literature readings are intended to introduce students to the lives of people who endured the Depression, the Dust Bowl, and the desperation of this era. The language arts, social studies, science, P.E., and mathematics activities are designed to help students recognize and empathize with the problems ordinary people faced during the Great Depression. The culminating activities aim to acquaint students with some of the aspects of Depression life that are not always fully understood by students today.

Enjoy using this book with your students. Look for other books in this series.

". . . farmers find no markets for their produce, the savings of many years in thousands of families are gone. More important, a host of unemployed citizens face the grim problem of existence, and an equally great number toil with little return."

Franklin Delano Roosevelt, 1933

Teacher Lesson Plans for Reading Comprehension

=========================== **Causes of the Depression** ===========================

Objective: Students will demonstrate fluency and comprehension in reading historically based text.

Materials: copies of Causes of the Depression (pages 7 and 8); copies of Causes of the Depression Quiz (page 19); additional reading selections from books, encyclopedias, and Internet sources for enrichment

Procedure

1. Reproduce and distribute Causes of the Depression. Review pre-reading skills by briefly reviewing the text and encouraging students to underline, make notes in the margins, list questions, and highlight unfamiliar words as they read.

2. Have students read the article independently, in small groups, or together as a class.

3. As a class, discuss the following questions or others of your choosing.

   • Which was the most important cause of the Great Depression?

   • Why was it unwise to buy stocks on margin?

   • How could future depressions be prevented?

Assessment: Have students complete the Causes of the Depression Quiz. Correct the quizzes together.

=========================== **Effects of the Depression** ===========================

Objective: Students will demonstrate fluency and comprehension in reading historically based text.

Materials: copies of Effects of the Depression (pages 9–11); copies of Effects of the Depression Quiz (page 20); additional reading selections from books, encyclopedias, and Internet sources for enrichment

Procedure

1. Reproduce and distribute Effects of the Depression. Review pre-reading skills by briefly reviewing the text and encouraging students to underline, make notes in the margins, list questions, and highlight unfamiliar words as they read.

2. Have students read the article independently, in small groups, or together as a class.

3. As a class, discuss the following questions or others of your choosing.

   • What was the worst effect of the Depression?

   • Should people have been ashamed of accepting charity? Why or why not?

   • What would you have done if you had lived during the Depression years?

Assessment: Have students complete the Effects of the Depression Quiz. Correct the quizzes together.

Teacher Lesson Plans for Reading Comprehension *(cont.)*

The Dust Bowl

Objective: Students will demonstrate fluency and comprehension in reading historically based text.

Materials: copies of The Dust Bowl (pages 12–14); copies of The Dust Bowl Quiz (page 21); additional reading selections from books, encyclopedias, and Internet sources for enrichment

Procedure

1. Reproduce and distribute The Dust Bowl. Review pre-reading skills by briefly reviewing the text and encouraging students to underline, make notes in the margins, list questions, and highlight unfamiliar words as they read.

2. Have students read the article independently, in small groups, or together as a class.

3. As a class, discuss the following questions or others of your choosing.
   • How would you have tried to put up with dust storms?
   • What choices did people have who lived in the Dust Bowl?
   • What personal lessons did you learn from the reading?

Assessment: Have students complete The Dust Bowl Quiz. Correct the quizzes together.

Education During the Depression

Objective: Students will demonstrate fluency and comprehension in reading historically based text.

Materials: copies of Education During the Depression (pages 15 and 16); copies of the Education During the Depression Quiz (page 22); additional reading selections from books, encyclopedias, and Internet sources for enrichment

Procedure

1. Reproduce and distribute Education During the Depression. Review pre-reading skills by briefly reviewing the text and encouraging students to underline, make notes in the margins, list questions, and highlight unfamiliar words as they read.

2. Have students read the article independently, in small groups, or together as a class.

3. As a class, discuss the following questions or others of your choosing.
   • Why did so many children miss school during the Depression?
   • How did the loss of schooling permanently affect these children?
   • What lessons can be learned from the way migrant children were treated in California?
   • What would you do if you were prevented from attending school?

Assessment: Have students complete the Education During the Depression Quiz. Correct the quizzes together.

Teacher Lesson Plans for Reading Comprehension *(cont.)*

The New Deal

Objective: Students will demonstrate fluency and comprehension in reading historically based text.

Materials: copies of The New Deal (pages 17 and 18); copies of The New Deal Quiz (page 23); additional reading selections from books, encyclopedias, and Internet sources for enrichment

Procedure

1. Reproduce and distribute The New Deal. Review pre-reading skills by briefly reviewing the text and encouraging students to underline, make notes in the margins, list questions, and highlight unfamiliar words as they read.

2. Have students read the article independently, in small groups, or together as a class.

3. As a class, discuss the following questions or others of your choosing.

   - Which agency of the New Deal do you think was most important? Why?

   - Why do you think President Roosevelt called closing the banks a "bank holiday"?

   - What New Deal ideas, programs, or projects are still in effect today?

   - Why was President Roosevelt's attitude important in combating the Depression?

Assessment: Have students complete The New Deal Quiz. Correct the quizzes together.

Reading Passages

Causes of the Depression

The *Great Depression* was a world-wide economic disaster that lasted from 1929 until 1942. It was the greatest economic disaster in modern times and affected the lives of most people in the industrialized nations of the world. Its effects on the United States were overwhelming.

Boom to Bust

The 1920s was regarded as an era of prosperity for most people in the United States. World War I had ended, and America had become a major world power. Most businesses seemed to be thriving, and businessmen were respected as the true leaders of the country. In fact President Calvin Coolidge said, "The business of America is business," meaning that everything else was less important.

Farm Failures

Underneath this apparent business boom, however, were some major problems. Farmers were not sharing in the general financial success. They were producing large crops, but the prices paid for farm products actually fell 40 percent. Many farmers were forced off their farms because they were unable to make the loan payments they owed to the banks.

Bank Failures

Although some banks were very successful, there were many bank failures. These failures occurred when a bank could not pay back the money that its customers had on deposit. More than 550 banks closed—mostly in agricultural areas—because the loss of farm jobs and lower prices made the economies of these communities very shaky. People who had savings in these failed banks usually lost everything.

Lower Wages

Another weakness of the 1920s boom was low pay for many factory workers. While a few businesses like Henry Ford's automobile factories paid good wages, most factory workers were not well paid. Owners tried to squeeze every dollar of profit out of their businesses. Competition from immigrants and Southern blacks moving to the North and West made it easy for factory owners to keep wages low. Workers had to cut their personal spending in order to survive, and businesses could not sell products to people who could not afford to buy them.

Reading Passages

Causes of the Depression *(cont.)*

The Stock Market Boom

Much of the growth of the 1920s business boom was based on speculation by individuals, banks, and businesses. People kept investing money in the stock market believing that the value of the stocks was going to keep going up. They expected to get rich quickly from these investments. Speculators tended to ignore instances where a company's stock suddenly lost value and the company went out of business, making that stock worthless.

Even more dangerous was the widespread practice of buying stocks *on margin*, where people borrowed money to buy the stock believing they could sell it at a higher price and make a profit without using their own money. From 1925 to 1929 the average price of stocks on the New York Stock Exchange doubled. The value of stocks was artificially high, however. Stocks were not actually worth the amount that they were being sold for.

The Crash of 1929

In late October 1929, the practice of speculating and buying stocks on margin ended with a massive crash of stock values. A Black Thursday (October 24) followed by an even worse Black Tuesday (October 29) destroyed the artificial values of stocks and led to a long period of falling prices over the next three years. Many stocks became worthless, and thousands of people who had invested in them lost their entire life savings. Banks and business speculators went bankrupt. People who had borrowed money to buy stocks lost everything they owned, including businesses, homes, cars, furniture, and even clothes. Millions of people lost their jobs and could not find work.

An International Depression

Throughout the world businesses failed, and people were thrown out of work. The United States passed the Smoot-Hawley Tariff Act of 1930 to protect American businesses from foreign competition by raising the taxes on products imported from other countries. This caused other nations to pass similar tariffs, which only reduced opportunities for people around the world to sell their products to other countries. These tariffs led to further unemployment and business failures worldwide.

 Reading Passages

Effects of the Depression

The economic collapse created by the Great Depression had a major impact on the lives of most Americans. Rising unemployment, low wages, limited opportunities for those who did have jobs, and the widespread suffering of so many people during the 1930s made people reevaluate their lives as well as the role of the government.

Lost Savings

People who had savings in the banks were forced to withdraw their money in order to pay off their debts, make the payments on their houses and cars, or simply to buy food. Many banks lost huge sums of money in the stock market crash and could not meet the demands of their customers who wanted to withdraw their money from their accounts. About 9,000 banks failed in the three years after the stock market crash, leaving millions of customers without any of their savings. Businesses and individuals could not borrow money, which made it even harder for businesses to function. Within three years the total value of goods and services produced in the United States fell from $104 billion dollars to about half of that amount.

Unemployment

For many families during the Depression years, the loss of the father's job was the start of a long descent into poverty, homelessness, starvation, and hopelessness. In 1925 the unemployment rate had been a low three percent. After the stock market crash of 1929, the unemployment rate jumped to nine percent in 1930 and shot up to 25 percent by 1933. In previous depressions, business had begun to pick up again in a year or two. This time the situation got worse instead of better.

At least 13 million American workers could find no jobs at all. Millions of men who still had jobs were forced to accept salary cuts which reduced their income by 20% or more. Millions of others took any low-paying or temporary jobs they could find, even though the future of these jobs was uncertain. Young people entering the job market—even those with a good education—took any job they could find, and often they could find nothing.

Thousands of men and children tried to make a living shining shoes or selling apples on city streets. A few people who could find no jobs turned to theft or other crimes in order to feed their families. Some teenage boys and girls went to live in the homes of families who needed farm help or help with housework or tending young children. They were paid only with food and a place to sleep. Women who wanted to enter the job market were at a disadvantage because an effort was made to hire men who had families to support, rather than women. Immigrants and blacks were especially hurt by the economic disaster.

 Reading Passages

Effects of the Depression *(cont.)*

Riding the Rails

Tens of thousands of teenage boys and a few girls, some as young as 14, left home in order to reduce the financial burden on their parents. It meant fewer mouths to feed in the family. These youth walked or hopped onto freight trains, heading to other communities to look for work. Since almost every town in the U.S. was affected by the economic collapse, they usually had a hard time finding even occasional odd jobs.

Those who regularly rode on freight trains were called *hoboes*, and their mode of travel was called "riding the rails." There were also many older men who rode the trains looking for work. In fact, sometimes there were more penniless hoboes riding the train than paying customers in the passenger cars. There were nearly a quarter of a million of these people in 1932.

Gaycats and Dingbats

Because they could not afford to pay for a ticket, hoboes learned how to jump on and off railroad boxcars, often while the train was moving. They could be arrested and jailed by the police or railroad cops who patrolled the railroad yards. Experienced hoboes were called *dingbats*. New hoboes were called *gaycats*. Many of these desperate men were crushed beneath steel train wheels when they missed a jump. It was a dangerous way to travel.

In some cities, hoboes had makeshift camps called *jungles* that were located near the railroad tracks. They built shelters out of cardboard boxes, broken furniture, discarded automobiles, and tree branches. At these camps, hoboes shared meals and slept.

Hoovervilles

Millions of people lost their homes in the Great Depression. Some lost their jobs and could no longer make the house payments to the bank on their loans so their homes were sold at auction. Others lost their jobs and could not afford rent for even the cheapest, most rundown house or apartment.

Families moved in with relatives when they could, but many families had no one to help them. These people ended up living in shacks made from cardboard, discarded wood, scrap metal, and any other materials they could find. They sometimes lived in rusted-out, abandoned automobiles. Many of these shacks were built at the edges of towns, often near a town dump where people could search for food, clothing, and trash which had been thrown away. These neighborhoods of broken down shacks were called *Hoovervilles*, a reference to President Herbert Hoover. Many people felt that Hoover had not done enough to help ordinary people deal with the economic difficulties they were facing.

President Herbert Hoover

 Reading Passages

Effects of the Depression (cont.)

The Necessities of Life

Food was cheap if you had the money, but many people were so poor that starvation and malnutrition were common. Mothers often made soup with whatever they had available. A soup bone, some cabbage, and a few spoiled potatoes had to feed whole families. Although farmers were dumping milk, burning crops, and killing hogs and cattle because prices were so low, children in the United States were regularly going to bed hungry.

Clothes were cheap, too, but not if you had no money. Mothers saved every scrap of cloth and used it to make children's clothes. Many used animal feed sacks and burlap bags to make dresses, trousers, shirts, and underwear. Many children went barefoot, even in the winter. Others shoved scraps of cardboard into the soles of their worn-out shoes. Newspapers, called *Hoover blankets*, were often used to keep warm at night, especially by the very poor.

Trying to Help

In the later years of the Depression, the federal government bought farmers' goods and gave them to distressed families, but at first the only help people received was from churches, local charities, and the Red Cross. All of these organizations were soon overwhelmed by the needs of the local communities and simply unable to help all the needy people.

Bread Lines

The winter of 1932–1933 was the lowest point of the Great Depression. The

Depression had been going on for more than three years, and many Americans were beginning to lose hope. The *bread lines*, which characterized the Depression, were the longest. Because so many people were out of work and had no money, the only way to avoid starvation was a bread line. Churches, private charities, and some communities set up soup kitchens to feed these destitute men, women, and children. Even Al Capone, an infamous Chicago gangster, financed a soup kitchen.

The food was simple and often consisted of oatmeal or bread for breakfast and bread and soup for dinner. Many bread lines and soup kitchens could only served a limited number of people, and those who were late were turned away.

The Shame of Poverty

In the 1920s and 1930s accepting charity from others was considered terribly shameful. Parents—especially fathers—felt that their failure to find work and provide a living reflected badly on them. They blamed themselves for the failure of the system. The fact that millions of people around the country and the world were also suffering did not lessen their sense of personal failure.

Many would not take charity from local groups, the government, or churches despite their families' needs. Others accepted help but felt forever scarred by their need. Some fathers even committed suicide out of a deep sense of shame.

 Reading Passages

The Dust Bowl

The Great Plains

The people living on the Great Plains—from the province of Saskatchewan in Canada south through Montana, North and South Dakota, Nebraska, Kansas, Wyoming, Colorado, Oklahoma, and Texas—took a double hit during the Great Depression. Farmers had plowed under the tough prairie grasses which for thousands of years fed the native buffalo of the plains. In place of these grasses, they planted wheat which grew well but needed plenty of rain and good soil to produce bumper crops. Wheat did not hold the topsoil well, and the land was easily eroded by wind and water.

Drought and Insects

Between 1931 and 1937, the Great Plains was hit by a long and brutal drought with virtually no rain. Farmers planted seeds and desperately hoped for rain. The little rain there allowed crops to start growing, but the plants then withered from a lack of more rainfall. Sometimes only a few seeds sprouted, and there were no roots to hold the loose topsoil so the plants could grow. Southern Kansas, the panhandle of western Oklahoma, and northern Texas were especially hard hit and became known as the *Dust Bowl*.

An insect invasion caused even more problems for farmers. Swarms of grasshoppers swept across thousands of acres, eating every plant in their path and even clothes hanging on the wash line to dry.

Black Blizzards

The wind usually blows a lot on the plains, but during the Dust Bowl years, there were terrible dust storms called *black blizzards*. The dust would blow at tremendous speeds and pile up in huge dunes next to houses, barns, and trees. Sometimes the loose dirt buried fences which were six feet high. The endlessly blowing dust seeped into every house through cracks in doors, windows, or boards. Everything inside became covered with a layer of fine dirt. At mealtimes glasses of water or milk had to be covered, or dust would turn the drinks brown. People even covered their food as they ate. People would wake up in the morning and see their pillow covered with a thick layer of dust except where their head had laid. Children and adults covered their faces with wet cloths to help them breathe during these terrible storms.

The wind stripped away the topsoil, making the land on the plains much less fertile and less likely to nurture crops when rain did come. The soil from the plains blew all the way to the Atlantic Ocean, where it even covered ships at sea. Farmers tried to protect their cattle, chickens, and other animals from the dust, but barns were no protection. Most farmers had animals that died or became sick by breathing dust and eating poor food. Farmers and their families gathered weeds and wild plants to try to provide some moisture for their animals. Cows that survived often provided very little milk because of the poor nourishment.

Reading
Passages

The Dust Bowl *(cont.)*

Buried Dreams

Many homes had to be shoveled out because the dust was so thick. Brooms could not move the thick piles of dirt. Fences had to be dug out and replaced. Entire farms and towns were buried in mounds of dirt. Cars, horses, cattle, and wagons were often buried. Some children and older people got lost in the storms and died. Unable to grow crops, many farmers lost their farms to the banks that held the loans on the land and buildings.

On the Move

Tens of thousands of families were forced to leave their farms and travel elsewhere to live. Some went to live with relatives, but most families loaded what few possessions they still owned and tried to find work. Over 2½ million people left their homes on the plains. Some went to Idaho, Oregon, and Washington. Some wandered through the Midwest or headed east hoping for work or even an occasional job for a day or two.

Some families traveled by horse and wagon. A few families had old *jalopies*, broken-down cars or trucks, on which they loaded their possessions. Many had nothing but hand carts or children's wagons to carry their clothes and belongings. They walked and pulled or pushed these carts and wagons.

The Great Migration

People from Oklahoma and Texas especially struggled to survive. Over one million people headed for California, where they hoped to find jobs working on farms or picking crops. They traveled across the southwestern states to California any way they could. Those with vehicles drove until they ran out of gas and then waited until kind strangers drove by and let them take a few gallons of gas out of their tank. Sometimes an entire family would push its old truck, car, or wagon up hills and along roads. Other people walked or got occasional rides from strangers as they headed west.

These travelers kept clean as best they could by washing in ditches. In order to survive they ate coffee grounds, carrot tops, apple cores, and garbage they got from farms or town dumps along the way. They were poor and desperate, and many communities just wanted them to move on. This was one of the largest migrations, or movement, of people across the country in American history.

The Dust Bowl *(cont.)*

Moving West

When these weary travelers reached the West, they tried to start over. In Oregon they cut trees. In Washington they helped build dams. In Idaho they settled on abandoned land.

In California these families camped wherever they could. They made shacks of cardboard and tin, slept under bridges, or camped in the bottoms of dry rivers or lakes. California offered few opportunities. Some families were able to find work as migrant laborers, picking crops for large produce farms. They faced competition from Mexican and Japanese migrant workers as well. An entire family sometimes made only a few dollars a week.

Most of these people had no place to go, no food for their families, no gas for their vehicles, and no hope for work. Children lived on lard sandwiches, boiled cabbage, and corn bread if they were lucky. The water supply, whether from streams or ditches, quickly became polluted because it was used for drinking, washing clothes, bathing, and a toilet.

Contagious diseases and infections were very common. Mosquitoes and other insects spread disease too. During the rainy season, the camps were muddy and filthy. Many children and older people died from malnutrition, illness, and injuries.

A few migrants returned to the Dust Bowl, but most stayed in the West and hoped for the best. The federal government's efforts to end the Depression gave many of these people a chance at a new life. The *New Deal* (see pages 17 and 18) that President Franklin D. Roosevelt set up finally offered hope for these migrants.

Reading Passages

Education During the Depression

School Taxes

The education of young children was severely affected by the Great Depression. Schools were paid for from local property taxes on homes and businesses. So many businesses and factories were closed and so many people lost their homes that tax revenues in local communities were often cut by more than half. There was no help available from the federal government, and the states had even less tax money to work with.

Cutting Expenses

Local school districts did everything they could to cut expenses. They hired fewer teachers and put more students in classrooms, sometimes as many as 50 or 60 in one class. Desks and textbooks were not purchased. Many children sat on the floor or shared a desk and a chair. Children shared textbooks and often used old or torn books. Kindergartens were cut from schools.

In small towns, children attended a one-room schoolhouse where one teacher taught all ages from six to 15 as well as taught all subjects. Special classes such as home economics, physical education, and foreign languages were cut to save money. Teachers concentrated on reading, writing, and arithmetic at both the elementary and high school levels.

School nurses were not rehired even though many children were suffering from disease, infection, and severe malnutrition caused by a lack of proper food. Most children never saw a doctor to get medical treatment, and the lack of school nurses only made the spreading of contagious diseases worse.

Missing School

Many children simply could not afford to attend public school. Parents could not buy decent clothes for their children. Some students who did attend school wore rags, shirts or dresses made from sacks, and worn-out coats.

Schools often required students to furnish their own school supplies, which caused many children to drop out of school. Families had no money for food, let alone school supplies, so some children never went to school—even in the earliest grades.

1700   1750   1800   1850   1900   1950

 Reading Passages

Education During the Depression *(cont.)*

Interrupted Schooling

Many children in grades four through eight missed school because they had to stay home and care for younger children. Others worked on farms to help the family survive. Some families became migrant farm workers, and even the youngest children picked crops to add to the family income. Sometimes there was no school to attend.

Many schools closed early every year or opened for only two or three months in the winter. By 1933 many public schools were closed, and at least three million children had no school to attend. Many students did not attend high school.

Teachers

More than 7,000 teachers lost their jobs during the Great Depression. Thousands of others barely made ends meet. Most teachers endured severe cuts in pay and had few if any benefits. More women teachers were hired because they could be paid less than men for doing the same job. Classes increased in size, and teachers were not paid if school was closed early.

Some districts were so strapped for cash that they paid teachers in *scrip*, a form of local paper money which could only be spent in local stores. In some rural districts, teachers lived in the schoolhouse and cooked their meals on the wood stove. Their pay was only a place to live and donated food.

Dust Bowl Children in California

Migrant children from the Dust Bowl who went to school in California were at a severe disadvantage. They had missed a lot of school at home and lost more on the journey west. They were often tired and listless at school because they had such poor nutrition, and some children had trouble staying awake in class.

These children were considered difficult to teach and either lazy or stupid. Some people thought these children were mentally retarded. Children from Oklahoma and Texas spoke with accents that were hard for many California teachers and students to understand. Local children teased them because of their clothes, looks, accents, and poor achievement in school.

Okies

So many people migrated from Oklahoma that they were referred to as *Okies*. The term was often used in a negative way and implied that these migrants were poor, lazy, and uneducated. The images of people from the Dust Bowl were further reinforced in John Steinbeck's classic book *The Grapes of Wrath*, songs by Woody Guthrie, and photographs taken by Dorothea Lange. However, in recent years the term "Okie" has taken on a new meaning. It has become a badge of honor to many people from Oklahoma, a symbol of their ability to survive.

Reading Passages

The New Deal

Hoover's Policies

The Great Depression had severe, long-term effects on the lives of most Americans. Before the Depression, people believed that businesses would automatically provide good products and services at low prices without being regulated by the government. The collapse of the economy in 1929 made people realize that action was needed to correct the problems.

President Hoover strongly believed that the government should leave business alone and just let the Depression take its course. He did try to help businesses by pressing for higher tariffs to protect American businesses from foreign competition. This policy backfired, however. It led to high tariffs in other countries, which made it difficult for American businessmen and farmers to sell their products to other countries.

Hoover was able to convince Congress to establish the Reconstruction Finance Corporation in 1932. This agency lent money to banks, railroads, and major corporations to prevent an even deeper economic collapse. But on the whole, Americans were unhappy with Hoover's approach, and in 1932 they elected Democrat Franklin D. Roosevelt as president.

The 100 Days

Franklin Roosevelt brought an energy and sense of hope to the nation. Roosevelt and his advisors believed the Depression could not be cured without strong intervention from the federal government. His inaugural speech set the tone for his administration. He declared that the only thing Americans had to fear was fear itself. To ease those fears, he set out to get Congress to act on a series of proposals in the first 100 days of his presidency. Roosevelt wanted to provide a "New Deal" for the American people.

Bank Holidays

One of the actions Roosevelt took was to close all of the banks in the United States, calling it a "bank holiday." Bank inspectors were brought in to examine the records of each bank, and only banks that were properly run were allowed to reopen. Roosevelt also convinced Congress to set up the Federal Deposit Insurance Corporation (FDIC) to regulate bank operations and insure bank deposits so that widespread bank failures would not occur again. The government wanted to guarantee that the money customers deposited in a bank insured by the FDIC was protected and would be available when needed.

The New Deal *(cont.)*

"Alphabet Agencies" Provide Relief

President Roosevelt recognized how desperate people were, and he worked to set up programs to help the needy. These programs, such as the CCC and WPA, were commonly referred to by the first letters in each word.

The Civilian Conservation Corps (CCC) was established to provide work for millions of unemployed young men. These men were paid to work on all types of conservation projects in local communities and on federally owned land. They planted trees, cleared underbrush, and built roads and dams.

The Federal Emergency Relief Act (FERA) was created to give money to states to be distributed to the needy. The Civil Works Administration (CWA) and the Works Progress Administration (WPA) were established by Congress to provide construction jobs for the unemployed and to build needed public facilities. Many existing post offices, government buildings, schools, dams, bridges, highways, sewer systems, water pipelines, and other projects in the U.S. were built in the 1930s by these agencies. Some *boondoggles*, or useless jobs, were also created to keep people employed.

National Recovery

Roosevelt wanted to encourage business as well as support a system of fair wages for workers. The National Recovery Act (NRA) was introduced to enforce fair hiring and labor practices and to encourage and support business activity. Businesses across America posted the NRA logo as a sign of their support.

The Agricultural Adjustment Act (AAA) limited farm production and was passed to help raise farm prices. The Tennessee Valley Authority (TVA) was established to help people in the rural areas of the South by building dams and providing inexpensive electricity to areas where electric power had not yet reached. These spending projects pumped money into the economy, which helped businesses and encouraged job growth.

Preventing Future Depressions

The National Labor Relations Board (NLRB) was started to protect workers from being treated unfairly by companies. It also helped struggling labor unions get the right to organize workers. The Securities and Exchange Commission (SEC) was created to protect investors from unfair or illegal actions by those selling stocks and bonds. The Social Security Act set up the first national retirement system for all Americans. Its main purpose was to make sure that people would have money to live on in their old age.

President Roosevelt's greatest accomplishment, however, was the sense of confidence he brought to America and his success at raising the nation's morale. His New Deal did indeed give Americans a sense that the future would be brighter.

Causes of the Depression Quiz

Directions: Read pages 7 and 8 about the causes of the Great Depression. Answer each question below by circling the correct answer.

1. In what year did the Great Depression begin?

   a. 1942
   b. 1829
   c. 1929
   d. 1932

2. Who did not share in the prosperity of the 1920s?

   a. farmers
   b. stock speculators
   c. factory owners
   d. businessmen

3. During the 1920s, most factory workers were

   a. overpaid
   b. women
   c. given health insurance
   d. not well paid

4. Who said that "the business of America is business"?

   a. Calvin Coolidge
   b. George Washington
   c. Henry Ford
   d. Franklin Roosevelt

5. People who invest money in the stock market to get rich quick are called

   a. tariffs
   b. industrialists
   c. speculators
   d. immigrants

6. Which business owner paid good wages to his factory workers?

   a. Calvin Coolidge
   b. Henry Ford
   c. Herbert Hoover
   d. Franklin Roosevelt

7. Problems that led to the Great Depression included

   a. low wages
   b. farm failures
   c. bank failures
   d. all of the above

8. What term means to buy stocks on borrowed money in the hope of selling at a higher price?

   a. on margin
   b. bond
   c. tariff
   d. competition

9. Which word means a tax on foreign products?

   a. import
   b. tariff
   c. export
   d. speculator

10. Competition from which group of people helped keep factory wages low?

    a. Southern blacks
    b. foreign immigrants
    c. businessmen
    d. both a and b

Effects of the Depression Quiz

Directions: Read pages 9–11 about the effects of the Great Depression on people's lives. Answer each question below by circling the correct answer.

1. What percentage of the U.S. population was out of work by 1933?

   a. 9%

   b. 25%

   c. 3%

   d. 13%

2. During the Depression, many people

   a. lost their jobs and homes

   b. saved their money

   c. invested in the stock market

   d. both a and c

3. What name was given to newspapers used as bedding?

   a. gaycats

   b. Hoovervilles

   c. burlap

   d. Hoover blankets

4. Why did farmers dump milk and kill hogs and cattle?

   a. prices were too high

   b. there was too much rain

   c. nobody wanted to buy them

   d. prices were too low

5. What did not happen in the U.S. during the Depression?

   a. many new factories opened

   b. banks closed

   c. people lost all their savings

   d. unemployment increased

6. Who were hit especially hard by the economic disaster?

   a. immigrants

   b. blacks

   c. women

   d. all of the above

7. How many banks failed in the three years after the stock market?

   a. 50

   b. 9,000

   c. 800

   d. none

8. What word was used to describe neighborhoods of cardboard shacks and rusted cars used as homes?

   a. Hoovervilles

   b. gaycats

   c. railroad boxcars

   d. immigrants

9. What word refers to homeless people who were "riding the rails" looking for work?

   a. speculators

   b. hoboes

   c. immigrants

   d. peasants

10. What were burlap bags and feed sacks used for by poor families?

   a. to cook dinner

   b. to cover their dogs

   c. to make clothes

   d. to make dolls

The Dust Bowl Quiz

Directions: Read pages 12–14 about the Dust Bowl. Answer each question below by circling the correct answer.

1. From 1931 to 1937 the Great Plains experienced
   - a. snowstorms
   - b. floods
   - c. drought
   - d. earthquakes

2. Which word means a long period with no rain?
   - a. blizzard
   - b. drought
   - c. bumper
   - d. erosion

3. What were black blizzards?
   - a. dust storms
   - b. hail storms
   - c. snowstorms
   - d. thunderstorms

4. In which state did migrants from the Dust Bowl sometimes get work picking crops on large farms?
   - a. Texas
   - b. California
   - c. Oklahoma
   - d. Idaho

5. What are *jalopies*?
   - a. migrant workers
   - b. hand carts
   - c. broken-down cars or trucks
   - d. horse-drawn wagons

6. How many people from the Great Plains left during the Dust Bowl years?
   - a. ½ million
   - b. 2½ million
   - c. 1 million
   - d. 9,000

7. How did the dust storms affect people and animals?
   - a. smothered them
   - b. killed the insects
   - c. made them sick
   - d. both a and c

8. What destroyed crops besides dust storms?
   - a. cows
   - b. thunderstorms
   - c. grasshoppers
   - d. lightning

9. Why was wheat bad for the soil?
   - a. it grew too tall
   - b. it did not hold the topsoil
   - c. it did not need rain
   - d. it was used to make bread

10. Which was not a problem found in migrant camps?
    - a. too much food
    - b. contagious diseases
    - c. polluted water
    - d. insects

Education During the Depression Quiz

Directions: Read pages 15 and 16 about education during the Great Depression. Answer each question below by circling the correct answer.

1. How were public schools paid for during the Depression?

   a. federal taxes
   b. state taxes
   c. local property taxes
   d. local sales taxes

2. What did school districts not do to cut expenses?

   a. close schools early
   b. raise taxes
   c. make classes larger
   d. close kindergartens

3. Which of the following became a problem because of the lack of school nurses?

   a. contagious diseases
   b. lack of exercise
   c. sick parents
   d. fewer textbooks

4. School districts hired more women teachers because

   a. they earned less pay
   b. they taught better
   c. men were too busy
   d. no one else wanted the job

5. Which is a reason some children did not attend school?

   a. they didn't like school
   b. they had to walk too far
   c. they didn't have decent clothes
   d. they were watering the crops

6. In the Depression years, many teachers

   a. lived in the school
   b. had their pay cut
   c. lost their jobs
   d. all of the above

7. What word means a form of paper money that can only be used in local stores?

   a. malnutrition
   b. scrip
   c. taxes
   d. migrant

8. During the Depression

   a. many teachers lost their jobs
   b. many students quit school
   c. many schools closed
   d. all of the above

9. Some California teachers thought the children of Okies were retarded because they

   a. were sleepy in class
   b. spoke with accents
   c. didn't learn quickly
   d. all of the above

10. Which of the following classes was not likely to be cut from schools during the Depression?

    a. home economics
    b. mathematics
    c. physical education
    d. foreign languages

The New Deal Quiz

Directions: Read pages 17 and 18 about the New Deal. Match the government program listed on the left with its correct description on the right.

Government Programs

_____ 1. AAA

_____ 2. CCC

_____ 3. FDIC

_____ 4. FERA

_____ 5. NLRB

_____ 6. NRA

_____ 7. SEC

_____ 8. Social Security Act

_____ 9. TVA

_____ 10. WPA

Descriptions

a. regulated banks and insured bank deposits

b. built post offices, bridges, schools, and other public buildings

c. hired young men to work on conservation projects

d. helped people in the rural South and generated electricity

e. established a national retirement system

f. protected workers from unfair treatment by companies

g. gave money to states to help the needy

h. limited farm production and helped raise farm prices

i. enforced fair hiring and labor practices

j. protected investors buying stocks and bonds

Teacher Lesson Plans for Language Arts

Vocabulary and Idioms

Objectives: Students will learn to apply their language arts skills in vocabulary enrichment and language usage.

Materials: copies of Great Depression Terms (page 26); copies of American Idioms (page 27)

Procedure

1. Reproduce and distribute the Great Depression Terms activity sheet. Review the vocabulary and pronunciation if necessary. Have students do the crossword puzzle independently.

2. Reproduce and distribute the American Idioms activity sheet. Explain the meaning and use of idioms, and give some examples. Have students complete the activity sheet independently.

Assessment: Correct both activity sheets with students. Review vocabulary and idioms as needed.

Literature

Objectives: Students will read and respond to novels with Depression-era subjects and learn about one author.

Materials: copies of *Soup for President* (page 28); copies of Focus on Author Robert Newton Peck (page 29); copies of the books *Soup for President* and other books by Robert Newton Peck listed in the Annotated Bibliography (page 45); dictionaries

Procedure

1. Read the book *Soup for President* as a class, in small groups, or independently.

2. Reproduce and distribute the *Soup for President* activity sheet. Have students answer the comprehension questions on their own. Allow them to share their answers with the class.

3. As a class or in small groups, review the discussion questions and vocabulary words on the activity sheet.

4. Reproduce and distribute the Focus on Author Robert Newton Peck activity sheet. Read the biographical information together.

5. Provide a variety of Robert Peck's books, including the Soup series, for students to read. Instruct them to choose and read one of these books.

6. Have students complete the assignment at the bottom of the page.

Assessment: Use written assignments and participation in class discussions to assess students' understanding of the literature read.

Teacher Lesson Plans for Language Arts *(cont.)*

Depression-Era Stories

Objectives: Students will read and respond to novels with Depression-era subjects.

Materials: copies of *Bud, Not Buddy* (page 30); copies of *Out of the Dust* (page 31); copies of Depression Stories (page 32); copies of the books *Bud, Not Buddy*, *Out of the Dust*, or other books listed on page 32 or in the Annotated Bibliography (page 45); copies of a dictionary and thesaurus

Procedure

1. Read the book *Bud, Not Buddy* as a class, in small groups, or independently.

2. Reproduce and distribute the *Bud, Not Buddy* activity sheet. As a class or in small groups, discuss the answers to the questions on the page.

3. Have students choose one of the extension activities at the bottom of the page. Allow them to share what they did with the class.

4. Have students read the book *Out of the Dust* as a class, in small groups, or independently. (**Note:** This is a book for ages 11–13.)

5. Reproduce and distribute the *Out of the Dust* activity sheet. As a class or in small groups, discuss the answers to the questions on the page.

6. Have students do the Extension activity, writing an essay about the Dust Bowl.

7. Reproduce and distribute the Depression Stories activity sheet. Have students read one of the books listed on the page. When finished, instruct them to complete the assignment.

Assessment: Use written assignments, participation in class discussions, and essays to assess students' understanding of the literature read.

Readers' Theater

Objective: Students will learn to use their voices effectively in dramatic reading.

Materials: copies of Readers' Theater Notes (page 33); Readers' Theater: West to Hope (pages 34 and 35); and Readers' Theater: Hooverville Blues (pages 36 and 37)

Procedure

1. Review the basic concept of readers' theater with the class, using the Readers' Theater Notes to emphasize important skills.

2. Have students read Readers' Theater: West to Hope and Readers' Theater: Hooverville Blues. Place students in small groups and allow time to practice reading the script over several days.

3. Schedule class performances, and have students share the prepared scripts.

4. As an extension, have students write and perform their own scripts about the Great Depression.

Assessment: Base performance assessments on the participants' pacing, volume, expression, and focus. Student-created scripts should demonstrate general writing skills, dramatic tension, and a good plot.

Great Depression Terms

Directions: After reading pages 7–18, complete the crossword puzzle below using the terms in the Word List. If needed, use the glossary on page 46 or a dictionary to help find the meaning of each word.

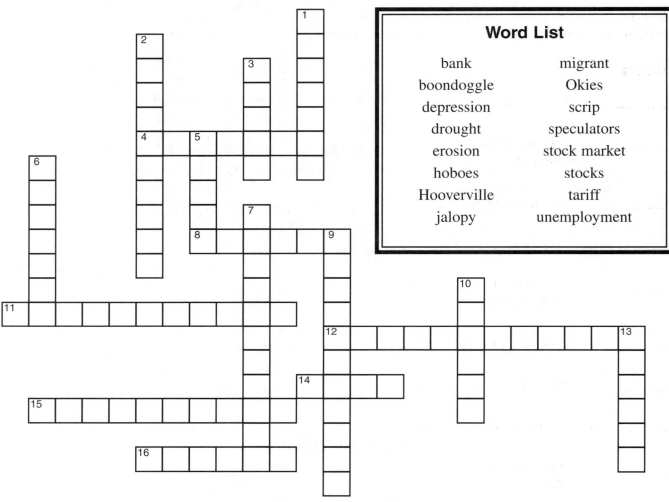

Word List

bank	migrant
boondoggle	Okies
depression	scrip
drought	speculators
erosion	stock market
hoboes	stocks
Hooverville	tariff
jalopy	unemployment

Down

1. a person who moves from place to place to find work
2. a difficult economic time with rising unemployment
3. a paper receipt used as money
5. people from Oklahoma and elsewhere who moved to California
6. long period with no rain
7. shacks and rusted vehicles where homeless people lived
9. people who gamble on stock values
10. a broken-down truck or car
13. a tax on imported products

Across

4. the wearing away of soil by wind or rain
8. shares of a company that can be bought
11. place where shares of a company are bought and sold
12. being unable to find work
14. place where money is saved or borrowed
15. meaningless work project
16. poor, homeless people who use to "ride the rails"

American Idioms

Speakers of American English use many *idioms*, or sayings that add "color" to our language. Often these sayings express an idea more effectively. For example, to say that a person is as "cool as a cucumber" is more expressive than to comment that a person is "calm."

Directions: Match the idioms with their meanings. Write the letter of the meaning in the column on the right on the blank line in front of the correct idiom on the left.

Idioms

_____ 1. Use more elbow grease.

_____ 2. Cross that bridge when you come to it.

_____ 3. Don't get your hackles up.

_____ 4. Every cloud has a silver lining.

_____ 5. Don't throw the baby out with the bath water.

_____ 6. I have an ax to grind with you.

_____ 7. You are going to eat crow.

_____ 8. You are skating on thin ice.

_____ 9. He is really hot under the collar.

_____ 10. He has bats in his belfry.

Meanings

a. Don't get upset.

b. Work harder.

c. Don't destroy the good with the bad.

d. Don't anticipate trouble.

e. Some good comes from every bad event.

f. You're going to be embarrassed.

g. He's crazy.

h. He's very angry.

i. I have a problem with something you said or did.

j. You are looking for trouble.

Extension

On a separate sheet of paper, draw a picture to illustrate one of the above idioms or another one of your choosing. Use colored pencils, crayons, or markers to color the picture. See if classmates can identify the idiom you drew.

Soup for President

Soup for President by Robert Newton Peck is set in Depression-era Vermont during the 1836 presidential election. While Franklin D. Roosevelt and Alfred M. Landon are competing for the White House, Luther Wesley Vinson (Soup) and Norma Jean Bissell are competing for class president at their school. Robert Peck is Soup's best friend, and Norma Jean is his girl. The story is fast-moving and funny.

Comprehension Questions

Read *Soup for President*. On a separate sheet of paper, answer the following questions.

1. Why did Robert take three whacks with the ruler instead of reading the note?
2. Why did Rob have red hands?
3. Who actually painted Soup's name on the barn?
4. Why did Miss Kelly need the boys to remove the paint from Mr. McGinley's barn?
5. Who is the best fullback in school?
6. What did the boys need the hair for in Mr. Petty's barbershop?
7. What song did Rob sing under Norma Jean's window?
8. Who was Soup's campaign manager?
9. Who won the election?
10. What book are students reading in Miss Kelly's class?

Discussion Questions

Discuss the following questions with your class or small group.

1. What advice does Miss Kelly give Rob about girls? What do you think of this advice?
2. Which presidential candidate is probably more popular in Vermont—Landon or Roosevelt? What evidence from the book supports your answer?
3. Why did Rob sing under Norma Jean's window?
4. What do you think of Miss Kelly's teaching style? What do you like or dislike?
5. Why does Rob believe that campaign managers do all the work?
6. Why did Miss Kelly admire Rob for not reading Norma Jean's note aloud?
7. What kind of vote does Miss Kelly need from the school board to get a new football?
8. Which character did you like best? Why?
9. Who did Rob vote for? Why?
10. Why is the class election so close?

Vocabulary

On a separate sheet of paper, write the meanings of the words listed below.

1. ballot
2. deface
3. deportment
4. hoosegow
5. nominate
6. unanimous

Focus on Author Robert Newton Peck

Robert Newton Peck writes funny books as well as sad ones. The Soup series (see the bibliography on page 45) contains some of the most hilarious stories in all of children's literature. Whether it is using a young tree to whip apples through the window of the Baptist Church, crashing into a Halloween party riding a runaway wheelbarrow, losing all of their clothes in a skinny-dipping escapade, or arriving at a Christmas party in an airborne sleigh, Soup and Rob find tons of trouble and readers get loads of laughter.

Robert Newton Peck was born February 17, 1928, on a Vermont farm near Lake Champlain. He grew up in the Depression years of the 1930s when nearly a third of the working men in the nation could not find work, many people were without homes and food, and President Franklin Roosevelt had been elected to get the country back to better economic times.

Peck was brought up in the unique religious tradition of the Shakers, who put great value on the simple life. His father was a butcher and farmer, but the family struggled to survive. Peck attended a one-room schoolhouse in his elementary years. This kind of school had children from first through the sixth grades in the same room. It was here that Robert met the real Miss Kelly, who clearly had an enormous impact on his life.

Robert's father died when he was young, and Robert became the man of the house. He had to care for his mother, his aunt, and the family home and farm. He left school about the age of 12 and went to work doing whatever jobs he could find—lumberman, butcher, and paper mill worker.

The story of his early life is told from a humorous perspective in the *Soup* books. Rob's free spirit, fondness for adventure, and personal friendships offer one aspect of his youth. The serious side of Peck's youth is portrayed in his first book, entitled *A Day No Pigs Would Die*. The sequel is entitled *A Part of the Sky*.

Assignment

1. Read one of the Soup books or *A Part of the Sky*.

2. Write a brief summary of the plot.

3. Describe two or three events in the story that were humorous, sad, or exciting.

4. Mention one or two clues in the story which suggest Depression times.

5. Share your observations with the class or small group.

Bud, Not Buddy

Bud, Not Buddy is a Newbery Award winning book with a unique style and plot. Written by Christopher Paul Curtis, the central character is Bud, a Depression-era orphan forced to leave his latest foster family and set out on a quest to find the father he has never seen. Using only the information from a handbill and getting help wherever he can, Bud finally finds a family—but not the one he expected.

Assignment

Read the book *Bud, Not Buddy*. Discuss the following questions as a class or in small groups.

1. What trouble does Bud have trying to jump onto a freight train?

2. How did the people in Hooverville treat the boys? Do they seem prejudiced against the boys?

3. Why did the police burn down Hooverville?

4. Did people seem more prejudiced against Bud's race or his poverty? (Give examples from the story to explain your answer.)

5. Why did some men join unions while others opposed them?

6. Why did Lefty Lewis give Bud a ride to Grand Rapids?

7. Which of Bud's Rules and Things made the most sense to you? Why?

8. Why didn't Herman E. Calloway accept Bud at first?

9. How was Bud treated by the band?

10. Which member of the band did you like best? Why?

11. How is Bud actually related to Herman Calloway?

12. What happened between Mr. Calloway and Bud's mother?

Extension

Choose one of the following activities to do.

- Write five of Bud's Rules and Things on a piece of paper. Give an example from Bud's experiences that illustrates the rule.

- Make your own list of Life Rules and Things.

- Make a list of the circumstances in *Bud, Not Buddy* which indicate the problems of living during a depression.

- Make a list of the characters in the book who showed kindness toward Bud or other people in the story.

- Make a dictionary of the terms used in the story that you did not know. Share your dictionary with the class.

Out of the Dust

Out of the Dust, written by Karen Hesse, is a story about a teenage girl living in Dust Bowl Oklahoma during the Depression years. This Newbery Award-winning novel describes one girl's struggle to find hope in the midst of the swirling blizzards of dust, poverty, and personal suffering. Written in first person, the reader gets a very personal view of life and death on the Great Plains.

Assignment

Read the book *Out of the Dust.* Discuss the following questions as a class or in small groups.

1. The story is written in free verse. Did you enjoy this style of poetry? Was it easy or hard to read?

2. What personal accomplishment is Billie Jo most proud of?

3. What do Billie Jo's mom and dad argue about?

4. Why does Mom feel so sad about the "Wild Boy of the Road"?

5. Who is responsible for the bad burning accident? (Give reasons to support your answer.)

6. Should Billie Jo blame herself?

7. Why did the father get drunk? How did you feel about that?

8. What comments in the book show how much Billie Jo misses her mother after her death?

9. How do the children react to the family living in their school?

10. How do Billie Jo and her father respond to each other in the years after her mother's death?

11. How do you think Mad Dog feels about Billie Jo?

12. Why does Billie Jo leave home and return?

13. Will Billie Jo play the piano again? Why or why not?

Extension

Read through the book and note all of the descriptions of dust storms, the damage they caused, and how people protected themselves and their property. Write an essay describing these terrible storms and what people did. Try to express a sense of the power of these storms and the frustration and hopelessness that people felt about them.

Read over your essay. Underline weak words. Use a thesaurus or dictionary to find stronger, more descriptive words for the storms and people's feelings. Check your first draft for spelling, punctuation, and capitalization. Write a final draft to share with the class.

Depression Stories

The books listed below are set just before or during the Depression era and reflect the hardships and disappointments of life during those years.

- *Agnes May Gleason* by Kathleen Duey is a story set on a Colorado farm during the darkest year of the Depression. The main character, Agnes, does the chores for her injured father and worries about her brother who has left home looking for work.

- *Christmas After All: The Great Depression Diary of Minnie Swift* by Kathryn Lasky is the story of one family during the Depression. Minnie, who wrote the diary, soon has another sixth grader for company when her family takes in an orphan cousin from the Dust Bowl.

- *The Secret School* by Avi is set in a poor farming community in Colorado just before the Depression, which was a very difficult time for farmers. The local one-room school is closed early which means the main character, 14-year-old Ida Bidson, cannot take the exams for entering high school. She and the rest of the students decide to keep school going with Ida as the teacher.

- *Treasures in the Dust* by Tracey Porter is written in two voices by 11-year-old friends, Annie and Violet. They endure the endless blizzards of the Dust Bowl and the hardship these storms caused to their families and communities. One girl dreams of being an archaeologist. The other travels to California with her family in the migration of Dust Bowl families.

Assignment

Read one of the books listed above or another that is set during the Depression era. List 10 important events in the story.

1. _____
2. _____
3. _____
4. _____
5. _____
6. _____
7. _____
8. _____
9. _____
10. _____
11. What was the most important event? _____

_____
_____
_____

Readers' Theater Notes

Readers' theater is drama without costumes, props, stage, or memorization. It can be done in the classroom by groups of students, who become the cast of the dramatic reading.

Staging

Place chairs, desks, or stools in a semicircle at the front of the class or in a separate staging area. Generally no costumes are used in this type of dramatization, but students dressed in similar clothing or colors add a nice effect. Simple props can be used but are not required.

Scripting

Each member of the group should have a clearly marked script. Performers should practice several times before presenting the play to the class.

Performing

Performers should enter the classroom quietly and seriously. They should sit silently without moving and wait with their heads lowered. The first reader should begin, and the other readers should focus on whoever is reading, except when they are performing. If desired, actors can use accents, mime, or movement to add a more dramatic effect.

Assignment

Read one of the readers' theater scripts in this book: West to Hope (pages 34 and 35) or Hooverville Blues (pages 36 and 37). Work with your group to prepare for the performances, and then share your interpretations of the scripts with the class.

Extension

Write your own readers' theater script based on one of the events listed below or another topic related to the Great Depression. Practice your script with classmates, and then perform it for the class.

- Choose a chapter or event from any of the Soup books or from *A Day No Pigs Would Die*, written by Robert Newton Peck.

- Create a script about the life of a child or family who lived through the Dust Bowl.

- Write a script based on the book *Out of the Dust* by Karen Hesse.

Readers' Theater: West to Hope

This script tells about life during the Great Depression. There are seven speaking parts.

Narrator: Black blizzards of dust have pounded the Oklahoma panhandle for five years. The Goodman family watched the crops on their prairie farm dry up and die because of the lack of rain. Their cattle and chickens ate weeds and smothered in the dust. Mr. Goodman lost his land to the bank when he could not make the payments on his mortgage. The family loaded their few remaining possessions on an old, broken-down jalopy with boards on the back to hold their suitcases and the children.

Dad: I hate to leave this farm, but we have no choice. I can't get work anywhere. Everybody here is as bad off as we are or worse. They say there's work in California. We just have to give it a try. We've got enough gas to get us to Route 66, I think.

Annie: How are we going to get there, Dad? We don't even have money for gas. Our food won't last us but a few days.

Mom: We'll hope in the Lord, Annie. You take care of your brothers James and Woody, and make sure they don't fall off.

Narrator: The family traveled along the dust-swept roads of western Oklahoma and into eastern New Mexico where they turned onto Route 66, the long road leading to California. Dad took out a piece of hose a few feet long.

Dad: We're out of gas and lucky we got this far. We'll push our jalopy along this level stretch and hope for a kind motorist to pass by.

Woody: Why does Dad grab that old hose every time someone passes?

Annie: He's hoping for a good samaritan. Maybe this car will have one.

Dad: Mister, I could sure use a few gallons of gas if you can spare it.

Traveler: I haven't much myself, but you can siphon out a couple of gallons with that hose. You folks look to be in worse trouble than I am.

Annie: Night's coming on, Dad. What will we do?

Dad: You kids can sleep by the side of this road. Your ma and I will share the cab. You kids check that field. There may be some roots left from the harvest. Maybe some stunted ears of corn got missed. Check in a ways. Anything near the road's gonna be long gone. Lots of folks like us have come before.

Readers' Theater: West to Hope *(cont.)*

Narrator: The family continued along Route 66, traveling a few miles a day. Soon they faced even greater trouble.

Dad: The left rear tire is shot. There's no tread left on the tire. I can't patch the tube any more. I've wrapped the tire with cloth, but you children will have to walk from now on. Ma, we've got to dump some of the things in the back just like we've seen other families do.

Mom: I hate to leave those two kitchen chairs. They're the only furniture we have left.

Dad: It can't be helped. You kids keep a sharp eye out for food. There might be rabbits or other critters we could snare. Look for birds, too. Woody, keep some stones in hand to chuck at anything you see. We're out of flour, and all that's left are two ears of corn. Look sharp.

James: Annie, I miss home. I even miss school.

Annie: Me, too. We hardly went this year because we couldn't afford the clothes and the supplies. I hated it when some of the girls laughed at my feed-bag dress and burlap jacket, but we're going to be way behind if we ever go back to school.

Narrator: The family continued its long trek westward going through New Mexico and Arizona, finally entering California. They were pushing their jalopy now with the kids taking turns steering.

Dad: There's a camp ahead with people and what looks like a ditch with water. We'll stop there and get the news. Maybe someone will have some food. There sure is a lot of coughing.

Narrator: They pitched camp and joined other families just as poor, starved, weak, and exhausted as they were. They used the water in the ditch to clean up, but it was already badly contaminated with the dirt and filth of those who had already been there. The news they heard was not good. Nobody had found steady work. Most of the children and older people were sick with typhoid, dysentery, and other diseases.

Dad: The news isn't good, but we aren't quitting. We're going to keep on traveling until I find a job or we run into the Pacific Ocean. Our only hope is out west. People from the county gave me a few gallons of gas so we'd keep moving. They don't want us here either.

Annie: I sometimes wonder if the whole world isn't broke and on the move. All we've seen is a river of misery. Well, maybe there's a rainbow somewhere. We'll keep looking for one.

Readers' Theater: Hooverville Blues

This script tells the story of a family whose lives have been changed by the Great Depression. There are eight speakers, but some readers could do two parts.

Narrator: The Rankin family has a new home. When Mr. Rankin lost his job in a factory making cloth, he couldn't pay the rent on their small apartment. Mr. Rankin was unable to find any other job. He tried shining shoes and selling apples, but every street corner in the city had someone already doing that. It is 1933, and the Depression has been going on for almost four years. The only place the Rankins could find to live was the Hooverville on the edge of their city. Mr. and Mrs. Rankin and their six children have scrounged together some cardboard trash and a few wooden boxes,

Dad: Well, Millie, we were lucky to find this old rusted-out car. It must have been sitting here for 10 years.

Mom: I cleaned what I could, John, but the rust is just everywhere. We'll put those pieces of cardboard the kids found on the seats so the children won't be poked by the rusty springs sticking out through the seats. At least it will stop the wind and snow. God knows, nothing will cut the cold of these winter nights.

Jerry: Mom, we found these old pieces of wood by the railroad tracks. We can brace them up against the car and weave the cardboard in between the wood.

Claire: Dad, I found some coal left along the tracks from the railroad engines. We couldn't take any more because the railroad police ran us off.

Mom: We can use it for cooking and a little warmth this evening. Janey found some flat stones and bricks we can heat up to keep our feet warm tonight.

Janey: I'm hungry. Isn't there anything to eat?

Mom: I know, child. We all are. We'll have to make do with what we have.

Narrator: As the family begins to build a fire, a neighboring couple comes from their cardboard box shack a few feet away.

Neighbor: Folks, we see that you're new here. We've been here five months now. You have some coal. We've got some cardboard scraps and trash from the dump to burn. We've a little food to share. The potatoes are soft and the apples are partly rotten, but we have some to share if you're of a mind to.

Mom: We'd be grateful for the food and the company, neighbor. We have a few coffee grounds, part of a cabbage that's pretty wilted and some carrot tops my oldest son found in someone's garden.

Readers' Theater: Hooverville Blues *(cont.)*

Claire: Do any of the kids here go to school?

Neighbor: No, the city fathers don't even want to admit we're here. We're an embarrassment. The cops have run us out several times, but folks just drift back and start over. After all, people have to get rid of their trash somewhere. We're just trash ourselves to some people.

Claire: I miss school. I miss my friends, the teacher, and my lessons.

Neighbor: Well, there's not much you can do about your friends or teacher, but young Ruthie Johnson on the other side of this Hooverville shantytown has a bunch of kids she reads with and teaches some figures to. They've got no paper or books, but she uses the dirt to teach letters and figuring. She'll help any child. Ruthie was a teacher who lost her job in this depression. Her husband was killed trying to jump a freight train.

Narrator: The oldest two Rankin boys show up with their arms full of newspapers and join the group, reaching hungrily for the soup their mother has made.

Richard: Mom, we found piles of these newspapers that people had thrown away in an alley. Most are clean and can be used to make Hoover blankets. We can burn the others.

Mom: Thank you, boys. These should help keep you kids a bit warmer tonight.

Neighbor: Have all the kids sleep tight together at night, and surround them with those Hoover blankets. They'll hold in their body warmth and keep the cold out.

Mom: I can't keep the children clean or clothed. I never thought I'd see the day I dressed my children in trash from the dump and feed bags from the store.

Neighbor: The worst problem is water. That ditch along the edge of camp is totally filthy. Have your kids drink snow for water when they can. At least it's clean.

Dad: Neighbor, do you think this depression will ever end? I'm afraid I'm going to lose my whole family. My two youngest kids are too skinny for words, pale as snow and always coughing.

Neighbor: I hope so. I'd like to see everybody get jobs and homes, and then I'd be glad to come burn this Hooverville to the ground.

Dad: The day that happens, I'll be here to lend you a hand.

Teacher Lesson Plans for Social Studies/Math/Science/P.E.

Using a Map

Objective: Students will learn to derive information from a map.

Materials: copies of Drought and Dust Map (page 40); additional resources for research such as books, encyclopedias, textbooks, atlases, almanacs, and Internet sites

Procedure

1. Review the Drought and Dust Map with students. Point out important features of the map to students.

2. Assign the map activities on the page.

Assessment: Correct the map work sheet with students.

Working With Statistics

Objective: Students will learn to derive information from maps and statistical data.

Materials: copies of Statistically Speaking (page 41); additional resources for research such as books, encyclopedias, textbooks, atlases, almanacs, and Internet sites

---

Depression Statistics

- Jobs lost between 1929 and 1933:
    - 3.4 million manufacturing jobs
    - 1.4 million wholesale and retail jobs
    - 688,000 construction jobs
    - 576,000 service jobs
    - 214,000 finance/insurance/real estate jobs
- Total unemployment in 1933 was 13 million workers, which was 25% of the work force.
- In 1929, 4.5 million passenger vehicles were built.
  In 1933, 1.1 million passenger vehicles were produced.
- In 1933, General Motors controlled 41% of automobile production, Chrysler controlled 25% of the market, and Ford controlled 21% of the market.
- In 1929, there were 509,000 houses built.
  In 1933, there were 93,000 houses built.
- In 1929, net income on a family farm averaged $945.
  In 1932, net income on a family farm averaged $304.

Procedure

1. Review Statistically Speaking and any necessary math concepts.

2. Assign the questions on the page.

Assessment: Correct and review the math problems. Check for understanding, and review basic concepts as needed.

1700   1750   1800   1850   1900   1950

Teacher Lesson Plans for Social Studies/Math/Science/P.E. *(cont.)*

Wind Erosion

Objective: Students will learn about wind erosion and build models demonstrating it.

Materials: copies of Wind Erosion (page 42); materials listed on page 42 including a 3"-deep plastic container, garden soil or planting mix; wheat or oat seeds, grass seed, electric fan, spray bottle and water

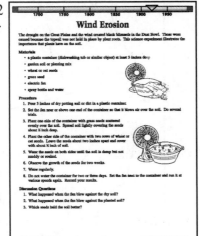

Procedure

1. Before beginning the project, collect the materials needed.

2. Reproduce and distribute the Wind Erosion activity page. Review the directions for making the model, and distribute the materials.

3. Allow students to demonstrate their completed models.

Assessment: Have students share their models with the class and discuss their results.

Tin-Can Stilts

Objective: Students will make a Depression-era toy.

Materials: copies of Tin-Can Stilts (page 43); materials listed on page 43 including 2 large food cans, strong string or twine, ruler or yardstick, hammer, large nail

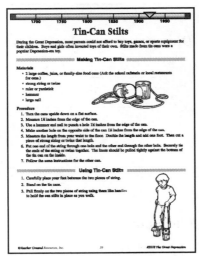

Procedure

1. Before beginning the project, collect the materials needed.

2. Reproduce and distribute the Tin-Can Stilts activity page. Review the directions for making the stilts, and distribute the materials. (**Note:** Adult supervision is needed for this activity.)

3. Have students try out their stilts in a suitable location. Allow plenty of space.

Assessment: Have students demonstrate their models for the class and discuss their ability to make their own toy.

Drought and Dust Map

The map below shows which U.S. states were affected by severe drought from 1931 to 1937. The Dust Bowl, the area with the most damage, is highlighted.

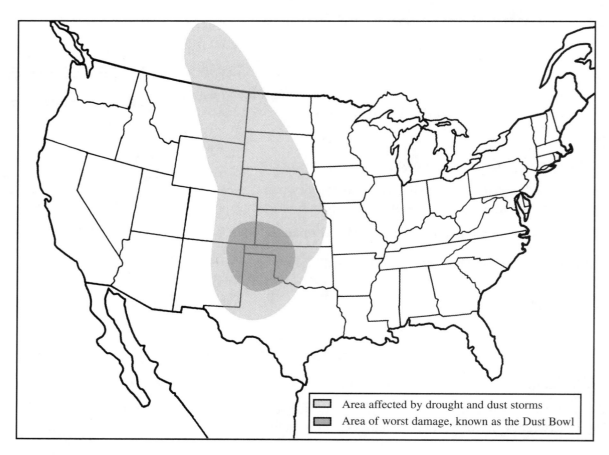

Area affected by drought and dust storms
Area of worst damage, known as the Dust Bowl

Directions: List the 10 states affected by the drought.

1. _____   6. _____

2. _____   7. _____

3. _____   8. _____

4. _____   9. _____

5. _____   10. _____

List the five states that made up the Dust Bowl.

11. _____   14. _____

12. _____   15. _____

13. _____

Statistically Speaking

Depression Statistics

- Jobs lost between 1929 and 1933:
    3.4 million manufacturing jobs
    1.4 million wholesale and retail jobs
    688,000 construction jobs
    576,000 service jobs
    214,000 finance/insurance/real estate jobs
- Total unemployment in 1933 was 13 million workers, which was 25% of the work force.
- In 1929, 4.5 million passenger vehicles were built.
    In 1933, 1.1 million passenger vehicles were produced.
- In 1933, General Motors controlled 41% of automobile production, Chrysler controlled 25% of the market, and Ford controlled 21% of the market.
- In 1929, there were 509,000 houses built.
    In 1933, there were 93,000 houses built.
- In 1929, net income on a family farm averaged $945.
    In 1932, net income on a family farm averaged $304.

Directions: Use the statistics above to solve the following math word problems.

1. How much did net family farm income decline between 1929 and 1932?_____

2. How many fewer houses were built in 1933 than in 1929? _____

3. How many more passenger vehicles were produced in 1929 than in 1933? _____

4. How many automobiles did General Motors build in 1933? _____

5. How many automobiles did the Ford Motor Company build in 1933? _____

6. If 13 million unemployed workers represented 25% of the work force in 1933, what was the total number of workers in the work force? _____

7. About what percentage of passenger vehicles were built in 1933 as compared to 1929?
    a. 25%   b. 50%   c. 75%   d. 90%

8. What was the total number of jobs lost in real estate, insurance, finance, services, construction, manufacturing, wholesale and retail employment between 1929 and 1933? _____

9. How many more manufacturing jobs were lost by 1933 than wholesale and retail jobs?
    _____

10. What percentage of the automobile market was not controlled by Ford, General Motors, and Chrysler? _____

Wind Erosion

The drought on the Great Plains and the wind created black blizzards in the Dust Bowl. These were caused because the topsoil was not held in place by plant roots. This science experiment illustrates the importance that plants have on the soil.

Materials

- a plastic container (dishwashing tub or similar object) at least 3 inches deep
- garden soil or planting mix
- wheat or oat seeds
- grass seed
- electric fan
- spray bottle and water

Procedure

1. Pour 3 inches of dry potting soil or dirt in a plastic container.

2. Set the fan near or above one end of the container so that it blows air over the soil. Do several trials.

3. Plant one side of the container with grass seeds scattered evenly over the soil. Spread soil lightly covering the seeds about ½ inch deep.

4. Plant the other side of the container with two rows of wheat or oat seeds. Leave the seeds about two inches apart and cover with about ½ inch of soil.

5. Water the seeds on both sides until the soil is damp but not muddy or soaked.

6. Observe the growth of the seeds for two weeks.

7. Water regularly.

8. Do not water the container for two or three days. Set the fan next to the container and run it at various speeds again. Record your results.

Discussion Questions

1. What happened when the fan blew against the dry soil?

2. What happened when the fan blew against the planted soil?

3. Which seeds held the soil better?

1700	**1750**	**1800**	**1850**	**1900**	**1950**

Tin-Can Stilts

During the Great Depression, most parents could not afford to buy toys, games, or sports equipment for their children. Boys and girls often invented toys of their own. Stilts made from tin cans were a popular Depression-era toy.

Making Tin-Can Stilts

Materials

- 2 large coffee, juice, or family-size food cans (Ask the school cafeteria or local restaurants for cans.)
- strong string or twine
- ruler or yardstick
- hammer
- large nail

Procedure

1. Turn the cans upside down on a flat surface.
2. Measure 1½ inches from the edge of the can.
3. Use a hammer and nail to punch a hole 1½ inches from the edge of the can.
4. Make another hole on the opposite side of the can 1½ inches from the edge of the can.
5. Measure the length from your waist to the floor. Double the length and add one foot. Then cut a piece of strong string or twine that length.
6. Put one end of the string through one hole and the other end through the other hole. Securely tie the ends of the string or twine together. The knots should be pulled tightly against the bottom of the tin can on the inside.
7. Follow the same instructions for the other can.

Using Tin-Can Stilts

1. Carefully place your feet between the two pieces of string.
2. Stand on the tin cans.
3. Pull firmly on the two pieces of string using them like handles to hold the can stilts in place as you walk.

Culminating Activities

Set aside one morning or day to devote to activities related to your study of the Great Depression.

Parent Help

Encourage parents or adult family members to help set up, monitor, and enjoy the activities. Check to see if they have any special talents, interests, or hobbies that would be a match for specific centers.

Eat Hearty

If you have adult volunteers, plan a luncheon with a country theme or one that highlights popular foods from the Depression era. Have students make table decorations at one of the centers. Make sure students do not have any food allergies or dietary restrictions.

Centers

The centers you set up should relate in some way to the Great Depression, daily life during that time, or activities from this book. Centers should involve small groups of six or seven students doing an activity and/or making something they can display. Each center should take about 20 minutes after which time students should rotate to the next activity. The following are suggestions for various centers. You may add others for which you have special expertise.

❑ **Readers' Theater**

This center involves practicing for a readers' theater presentation. Students can use a script in this book or one they wrote and then present it to parents or other classes.

❑ **Tin-Can Stilts**

Students can make tin-can stilts (page 43) and practice using them at this center.

❑ **Construct a Dust Bowl Farm**

Use construction paper, craft sticks, modeling clay, and other materials to construct a model of a Dust Bowl farm after a black blizzard. Add sand or fine dirt for the dust. Provide pictures from books and the Internet for reference.

❑ **Science Center**

Students can set up or extend the wind erosion experiment described on page 42. If desired, include models of water erosion as well.

❑ **Plant a Garden**

Students can plant a small vegetable garden. Use fast-growing seeds such as radishes, lettuce, beans, and peas.

❑ **Food and Toy Drive**

Collecting food for the needy was common during the Depression. Consider asking students to bring food or toy donations to donate to a local homeless shelter.

❑ **Games and Sports**

Play games and sports that were popular in the 1930s. For example, the board game Monopoly was created during the Depression-era by a man who was out of work. Baseball was the favorite sport; children used any ball and whatever they had available as a bat.

Annotated Bibliography

Fiction

Avi. *The Secret School*. Scholastic, 2001. (A tale set in farm country just before the Depression)

Curtis, Christopher Paul. *Bud, Not Buddy*. Random House, 1999. (A superb, middle-grade novel set in Depression-era Michigan)

Duey, Kathleen. *Agnes May Gleason: Walsenburg, Colorado, 1933*. American Diaries Series, Aladdin, 1998. (Interesting story of a girl having to take on adult responsibilities during a farmers' strike)

Hesse, Karen. *Out of the Dust*. Scholastic, 1997. (A Newbery Award-winning novel told in free verse, giving a first-person account of Dust Bowl suffering)

Lasky, Kathryn. *Christmas After All: The Great Depression Diary of Minnie Swift*. Dear America Series, Scholastic, 2001. (A fictional, realistic account of a child's response to hard economic times in Indiana in 1932)

Peck, Robert Newton. *A Day No Pigs Would Die*. Random House, 1972. (A classic account of Depression-era life in rural Vermont)

_____. *A Part of the Sky*. Knopf, 1994. (A sequel to *A Day No Pigs Would Die*)

_____. *Soup*. Knopf, 1974. (A humorous story set in Depression-era Vermont)

_____. *Soup and Me*. Knopf, 1975.

_____. *Soup for President*. Knopf, 1978.

_____. *Soup's Drum*. Knopf, 1980.

_____. *Soup in the Saddle*. Knopf, 1987.

_____. *Soup on Wheels*. Knopf, 1981.

_____. *Soup's Goat*. Knopf, 1987.

_____. *Soup on Ice*. Knopf, 1985.

_____. *Soup in Love*. Dell, 1992.

Porter, Tracey. *Treasures in the Dust*. Harper, 1997. (An excellent Dust Bowl story told in two voices)

Nonfiction

Coombs, Karen Mueller. *Children of the Dust Days*. Carolrhoda, 2000. (A beautifully illustrated lower-grade account of life in the Dust Bowl)

Grant, R. G. *The Great Depression*. Barrons, 2002. (A superb account of the Great Depression written for middle-grade students)

Graves, Kerry A. *Going to School During the Great Depression*. Capstone, 2002. (An outstanding account of school life during the Great Depression)

Press, Petra. *A Cultural History of the United States Through the Decades: The 1930s*. Lucent, 1999. (An excellent account of Depression-era life in the United States)

Ross, Stewart. *Causes and Consequences of the Great Depression*. Raintree, 1998. (A complete middle-grade account of the Depression from a worldwide perspective)

Stanley, Jerry. *Children of the Dust Bowl: The True Story of Weed Patch Camp*. Crown, 1992. (A story about life for Okies in a migrant labor camp)

Multimedia/Websites

Multimedia Collections: Roaring 20's & Depressing 30's (TCR 3039). Teacher Created Resources, 2002.

Weedpatch Camp. http://www.netxn.com/weedpatch

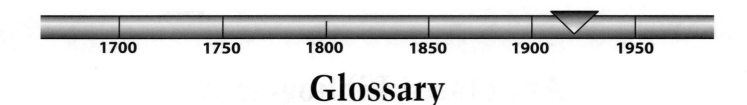

Glossary

bank failure—a bank cannot pay its depositors and goes out of business

bankrupt—the loss of all one's money and valuables

black blizzards—severe dust storms

blizzards—severe snow and ice storms

boom—successful economic times

boondoggles—useless work projects created by the government to give people jobs

bumper crop—very successful farm harvest

bust—a depression

depression—a severe economic downturn with many business failures and lost jobs

dingbats—experienced hoboes

drought—a severe shortage of rain

Dust Bowl—the hardest hit area of the Great Plains which included western Kansas, Oklahoma, and Texas

erosion—the wearing away of the soil by wind and rain

gaycats—new, inexperienced hoboes

Great Depression—the worldwide economic catastrophe lasting from 1929 until the early 1940s

hobo—a homeless wanderer

Hoover blankets—newspapers used as bedding

Hooverville—a shantytown of shacks and rusted vehicles where homeless people lived

jalopy—an old, broken-down truck or car

lard—cooking grease made from animal fat

margin—borrowing money to buy stocks

migrant—a person who moves from place to place doing seasonal or temporary jobs

migration—the movement of many people

morale—the spirit of a person or a people

New Deal—President Roosevelt's program for overcoming the Great Depression

Okies—people from Oklahoma and other Dust Bowl states who migrated to California

recession—a mild economic downturn

relief—food, money, and other help given to the poor

relief agency—a private or government group which helps the needy

rural—an area in farm country or small towns

scrip—a paper receipt for money which can only be redeemed in a local area

shanty—a shack

speculators—people who gamble on the value of a stock

stock market—place where shares in a company are bought and sold

stocks—shares of a company that people buy

tariff—a tax on products imported from other countries

topsoil—the fertile top layer of soil which helps crops grow

unemployment—not being able to find work

Answer Key

Page 19
1. c
2. a
3. d
4. a
5. c
6. b
7. d
8. a
9. b
10. d

Page 20
1. b
2. a
3. d
4. d
5. a
6. d
7. b
8. a
9. b
10. c

Page 21
1. c
2. b
3. a
4. b
5. c
6. b
7. d
8. c
9. b
10. a

Page 22
1. c
2. b
3. a
4. a
5. c
6. d
7. b
8. d
9. d
10. b

Page 23
1. h
2. c
3. a
4. g
5. f
6. i
7. j
8. e
9. d
10. b

Page 26
Down
1. migrant
2. depression
3. scrip
5. Okies
6. drought
7. Hooverville
9. speculators
10. jalopy
13. tariff

Across
4. erosion
8. stocks
11. stock market
12. unemployment
14. bank
15. boondoggle
16. hoboes

Page 27
1. b
2. d
3. a
4. e
5. c
6. i
7. f
8. j
9. h
10. g

Page 28
Comprehension Questions
1. He didn't want to embarrass Norma Jean.
2. He painted Soup's name on the barn.
3. Rob
4. Mr. McGinley was on the school board, and they needed his vote for a new football.
5. Janice Riker
6. for Soup's mustache
7. "My Country 'Tis of Thee"
8. Rob
9. Soup
10. *Ivanhoe*

Discussion Questions
1. Miss Kelly says to use poetry and music to court a girl. Answers will vary.
2. Landon is more popular because he is a Republican. Rob commented that most people in town "agreed that Democrat was a dirty word," and there were pictures of Landon all over town.

Answer Key (cont.)

Page 28 (cont.)

3. He was courting her.
4. Answers will vary.
5. He was the one who painted Soup's name on the barn.
6. It showed that he was noble and acted with honor.
7. She needs a unanimous vote.
8. Answers will vary.
9. He voted for Soup. Soup was his best friend.
10. The number of boys to girls in the class was about even, and both candidates were liked.

Vocabulary

1. ballot—piece of paper used to vote
2. deface—to damage or ruin a surface
3. deportment—behavior
4. hoosegow—jail
5. nominate—propose as a candidate for a job or office
6. unanimous—having everyone in agreement

Page 30

1. He is not experienced and was not able to jump on in time.
2. They are treated kindly. They do not seem prejudiced.
3. The police burned down Hooverville to run the poor people out of town.
4. Answers will vary.
5. Some saw unions as a way of keeping owners from mistreating them, and others saw unions as a threat to their jobs.

6. He felt sorry for him and thought he could help.
7. Answers will vary.
8. Calloway did not know who Bud was and thought he was trying to con him.
9. Bud was liked and well treated by the band members.
10. Answers will vary.
11. Herman is his grandfather.
12. Mr. Calloway and Bud's mother did not get along, and she left.

Page 31

1. Answers will vary.
2. Billie Jo is most proud of her ability to play the piano.
3. They argue about what to plant, how to farm, and money.
4. She feels sorry for him and his mother.
5. Answers will vary.
6. Answers will vary.
7. He could not take failure anymore. Answers will vary.
8. Billie Jo compares herself to her mother, often remembers her piano playing, and disliked the funeral because the minister did not mention her mother's special ways.
9. They accepted it and tried to help the family.
10. They do not talk much, and they both miss the mother and blame themselves for her death.

11. Mad Dog likes and admires her.
12. Billie Jo wants to get away from what is happening. She realizes home is where she belongs.
13. She probably will because playing the piano is her greatest skill and what she loves to do.

Page 40

1. Montana
2. North Dakota
3. South Dakota
4. Wyoming
5. Colorado
6. Nebraska
7. Kansas
8. New Mexico
9. Oklahoma
10. Texas
11. Colorado
12. Kansas
13. New Mexico
14. Oklahoma
15. Texas

Page 41

1. $641
2. 416,000
3. 3.4 million
4. 451,000
5. 231,000
6. 52 million
7. a. 25%
8. 6,278,000
9. 2 million
10. 13%